Kingdom Johnson

BAOFENG
RADIO
Handbook

for Beginners

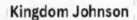

guide to
exploring Baofeng Uv-5r,
including troubleshooting

BAOFENG
RADIO
HANDBOOK
for Beginners

Guide to exploring Baofeng UV-5r, including troubleshooting

Kingdom Johnson

It contains only instructions for helping both beginners and pros explore exciting

Baofeng Radio features, programming,

and troubleshooting

Introduction

The Baofeng Uv-5r is a handheld radio that can be used to do a whole lot, from amateur radio to emergency communications. It is quite popular among users because it its affordability and multiple features, including the ability to store up to 128 channels, dual-band operation, and more.

However, programming and troubleshooting the Baofeng radio can be a bit challenging, especially for beginners. This book provides the needed help for new and experienced users to get the most out of their Baofeng Uv-5r.

TABLE OF CONTENTS

Introduction
1
Baofeng UV-5R Step-by-Step
Programming Guide. 8
2
Using Baofeng UV-5R As A Walkie
Talkie.......................................16
3
Tips And Tricks.........................24
Attaching Accessories....................26
How to Activate the Flashlight........27
How to Speak to Someone/Transmit
Information........,.........................28
How to Change Between Frequency and
Channel Mode...............................29
How to Change the Frequencies You're
Transmitting and Listening to.......... 31
How to Switch to a Different Channel............33

How to Enter a Frequency in Text................34

How to Change From VHF to UHF................36

How to Tune in to FM Broadcast................37

How to Switch Bands in FM Broadcast..........38

How to Modify Transmit Power................39

Raise Or Lower The Squelch Level................41

How to Secure a Keypad................42

How to Check Frequency................43

How to Modify Scan Preferences................45

How To Simultaneously Monitor Two Frequencies................47

How to Alter the Color of the Backlight..........49

How to Increase the Memory of the Radio's Frequencies................,................51

How to Get Rid of Saved Channels................54

How to Transmit a 1750 Hz Burst................55

Steps for Enabling Hands-Free Use................56

4

Troubleshooting BaofengbUV-5r Common Problems................58

5

Important Baofeng Accessories..........62

Programming Baofeng UV-5r

Baofeng UV-5R Step-by-Step Programming Guide

1. Set the radio to communicate with a repeater at 146.780– MHz, 100.0 Hz.

0. Make sure the radio is unlocked before turning it on.

1. The frequency mode VFO/MR

2. Choose the top display.

A/B

3. Change the frequency

1 to 4 to 6 to 7 to 8 to 0

4. Set the repeater offset to four.

MENU - 26 - MENU - 000600 - MENU - EXIT

5. Configure SFT-D, the repeater shift direction.

MENU - 25 - MENU - (minus) - MENU - EXIT

6. Set the T-CTCS transmit tone frequency.

MENU - 13 - MENU - 1000 - MENU - EXIT

7. Set the transmission power setting.

MENU - 2 - MENU - HIGH - MENU - EXIT

8. If desired, disable the TDR

MENU - 7 - MENU - OFF - MENU - EXIT

Your radio is now configured to transmit as indicated

2. Store the current repeater and tone settings in a memory channel.

0. To tune your radio to the frequency of your choice, follow the instructions above.

1. Delete the target memory channel.

MENU - 28 - MENU - 36 - MENU - EXIT

2. Put the frequency onto channel 36.

MENU - 27 - MENU - 36 - MENU - EXIT

press "receiving memory" to hear

MENU - MENU - MENU - EXIT

Press "transmitting memory" to hear it.

3. Recall a setting from a memory cache

1. Press VFO/MR (channel mode)

2. Then, press the up and down arrows channel number with three digits, all three digits

0 - 3 - 6

The stored channel is now ready for use

4. Set the radio for 147.480 MHz simplex communication

0. Start the radio and ensure that it is unlocked.

1. The frequency mode, or VFO

2. Choose the top display.

A/B

3. Change the frequency to 1 − 4 − 7 − 4 − 8 − 0

4. Deactivate SFT-D, the repeater shift direction.

MENU - 25 - MENU - OFF - MENU - EXIT

5. Choose the transmission power setting.

MENU - 2 - MENU - HIGH - MENU - EXIT

6. Optional: deactivate the TDR

MENU - 7 - MENU - OFF - MENU - EXIT

7. Clear memory channel 5 in the target.

MENU - 28 - MENU - 5 - MENU - EXIT

"Delete channel" is heard.

8. Keep track of the frequency in channel 5

MENU - 27 - MENU - 05 - MENU - EXIT

press "receiving memory" to hear

MENU - MENU - MENU - EXIT

Press to hear "transmitting memory"

Using Baofeng As A Walkie-Talkie

The initial step in two-way handheld wireless communication is simply to get a stylish walkie-talkie like a Baofeng gadget. Several Baofeng models are high-end hybrid devices, thus utilizing them can be challenging for beginners.

Many new users of the device wonder how to connect a Baofeng walkie-talkie to another radio. Fortunately, it's fairly easy to accomplish. This is advantageous since no one wants a product that makes them spend too much time figuring it out.

Today I'll write and discuss how to set up your BaoFeng to work with any FRS/GMRS 2-way handheld radio as well as how to link it to weather channels so you can receive weather alerts and messages.

You should be aware that in order to legally use the Baofeng, you require a GMRS license.

Activate the Baofeng. If your BaoFeng model has a speech feature, the voice of the device will indicate whether you are in "frequency" or "channel" mode.

Make sure the radio is on frequency move while it is turned on. Pressing the top left organs button will switch it to frequency mode if it is currently in channel mode.

Simply press the menu button in the frequency mode, followed by the '7' numeric button, to lock down the menu.

Use the down arrow to get to the power

setting in the menu and select a transmission power that complies with FCC regulations regarding the use of these walkie talkies without a license.

The Baofeng's maximum transmission power is 8 watts. One Watt is the least. Use the down arrow to change the power setting to low if it is already high.

Confirm the low power setting by hitting the menu button, and then press the exit button (next to the down arrow button on the right side of the device), to turn it off.

Choosing the channel you wish to broadcast on is the next step. To achieve this quickly, go to Google and type up "frequencies of FRS channels."

There would be a lot of webpages on the Google results page. You should be able to access any of the top websites on the first page. To access the FRS frequencies, simply click on any user.

As almost all websites show both GMRS and FRS frequencies, you want to make sure you select an FRS frequency if you're trying to connect the Baofeng to an FRS radio.

Once you've chosen a channel, write down or copy the frequency. Return to the Baofeng device and use the numeric keypad to enter the frequency while it is still in the frequency mode.

Now switch on the second walkie-talkie. Choose the same channel that you had set up in the Baofeng.

Depending on the kind of walkie-talkie you want to connect the Baofeng to, there are different ways to choose or change channels. Most handheld two-way radios have a dial at the top that may be turned to easily change channels while people are operating the radio.

You're done when you choose the same channel. Now that both walkie talkies are connected to the same frequency, they can talk to one another.

You might need to also enter the frequency number to match the frequency you programmed in the Baofeng if the second radio has a keypad.

Simply follow the directions above to connect the Baofeng walkie-talkie to the second Baofeng unit, and you're ready to go.

By pressing the PTT button on the other device and sending any message, you may verify that you are now connected. The speakers on the Baofeng would clearly hear you speaking.

When an incoming transmission is detected in Baofeng models like the UV-5RA, the display glows blue and the indicator below the power button turns green.

How to link weather stations to a Baofeng walkie-talkie

You must first be aware of the precise frequencies used by the local weather station. You could check out the nearest weather station's frequencies.

Make a frequency copy.

After that, just enter the Baofeng device's numeric representation of the weather station's frequency.

You could begin receiving signals from that weather station if you choose the correct frequency.

One advantage of Baofeng walkie talkies is that you may manually program these frequencies or use your laptop to do so, eliminating the need for frequency input each time you want to listen to a weather station.

Now you ought to have no trouble connecting your Baofeng walkie-talkie. Try your best to use technology wisely. The wise choice is to obtain a license if you wish to run the Baofeng at a greater transmission power outside in order to stay out of trouble with the FCC.

Tips And Tricks

How to Turn Your Baofeng UV-5R On

You only need to turn the knob next to the antenna at the top of the UV-5R radio to turn it on.

Attaching Accessories

A Kenwood 2-pin connection can be used to connect a variety of accessories to your UV-5R. Simply make sure that it works with a Kenwood 2-pin connector before spending any money on a headphone or other accessory for your UV-5R. Be cautious to turn off the radio first before connecting any accessories.

How to Activate the Flashlight

The UV-5R is equipped with a flashlight. I guess you could say it's a little like a Swiss army knife. On the left side of the radio, there is a "MONI" button that must be pressed in order to activate the flashlight.

How to Speak to Someone/Transmit Information

Once you've found the appropriate frequency (how to identify significant ham radio frequencies), press and hold the push-to-talk button on the side of your radio to make a contact. The largest button is that one. Keep the button depressed the entire time you speak, then release it after you finish.

How to Change Between Frequency and Channel Mode

Channel mode and Frequency mode are the two listening options available on your UV-5R. You can rapidly retrieve the frequencies that you've set your radio to remember by using channel mode. This speeds up listening to and transmitting on the frequencies that you frequently use.

In frequency mode, you can make precise adjustments to focus on a specific signal and scan frequencies to discover any incoming signals. It resembles the radio tuning dial in your car in certain ways.

You need to be aware of how to access both modes because they are both helpful. You must press the orange "VFO/MR" button on the radio's face to change between Channel Mode and Frequency Mode.

How to Change the Frequencies You're Transmitting and Listening to

You might occasionally want to transmit on one frequency while listening on another. This feature may come in handy if you end yourself acting as a message relay in a SHTF scenario. It could be that someone in a neighboring neighborhood needs to get in touch with someone else across the city, but they are too far away. Say your son requests that you let his girlfriend know that he is fine. He has no other method to get in touch with her because the cell towers are down. He can communicate with you, but he can't seem to get through to her.

This is where having such a function would be

useful. So, you must use the A/B button if you want to transmit on one frequency and then receive messages on another. By doing this, you can switch between the upper display and the lower display, which are both represented by the frequencies "A" and "B," respectively, at the top and bottom of the screen. As you look at these two frequencies, the frequency you are sending on is "B" at the bottom of the screen, while the frequency you are listening to is "A" at the top.

If you want to listen and transmit on the same frequency, you can leave both "A" and "B" at that frequency or you can switch one from the other. Everything is dependent upon your goals.

How to Switch to a Different Channel

If you've already loaded a number of frequencies into the UV-5R's memory, switching channels will make it easy to flip between them. Make sure you are in Channel Mode before you can do it. To accomplish this, press the "VFO/MR" button. Use the up and down arrow buttons to switch to the channel of your choice once you are in channel mode.

How to Enter a Frequency in Text

Let's say a friend provides you the radio station he likes to tune into in the morning. Although it isn't one of your saved channels, you want to check it out. You may rapidly access the correct frequency by typing it into the UV-5R keypad rather than slowly tuning your radio to it by using the up and down arrows.

To begin, you must be in frequency mode. By pressing the "VFO/MR" button, you can enter this mode. You can alter the frequency you're sending on and you can alter the frequency you're listening to on a UV-5R, which are two distinct features of frequency modification to keep in mind.

Second, click the "A/B" button to choose between changing the frequency you are sending from ("B" on the bottom screen) or the frequency you are listening to ("A" on the top screen). (If you're in UHF and want to program a frequency in VHF, or vice versa, you must press the "BAND" key after completing the previous step.)

Thirdly, you must type in the first three numbers of the frequency you want to listen to. As a result, the decimal's left-hand numbers will be filled in. To enter the four numbers on the right side of the decimal, round up to the next whole number. You must enter the final four numbers into the three places available, which are the only ones available. Entering 145.688 will allow you to listen to 145.6875, for instance. Now, the frequency you desired to listen to will appear on the screen.

How to Change From VHF to UHF

Dual-band transceiver is the term used to describe your UV-5R radio. It now has access to two separate bands, which is another name for a collection of radio frequencies. Imagine you have a friend who wishes to talk to you on UHF but your radio is currently tuned to VHF. The steps below should be followed if you want to change bands:

Make sure you are in frequency mode first. If you're in Channel Mode, you have to press the orange "VFO/MR" button on the radio's face. Hit the "BAND" key on the radio's right side once it is in frequency mode.

How to Tune in to FM Broadcast

Most people refer to "the radio" as Broadcast FM. This is the group of channels that you use to listen to music while driving. For instance, 94.6 can be a well-liked country music channel in your area. Your UV-5R can pick up these frequencies.

To make a call, you must press the orange "CALL" button on the radio's left side. Once broadcast FM is turned on, using the up and down arrows will let you to change the channel you're listening to. This will enable you to adjust the frequency to your desired level. You only need to press the "CALL" button one more to switch off broadcast radio.

How to Switch Bands in FM Broadcast

While listening to broadcast FM, there can come a point when you want to access a different band. You must first switch the radio to broadcast FM mode in order to achieve this. To achieve this, press the orange "CALL" button located above the push-to-talk button on the radio's left side.

When you press the "BAND" button on the radio's front face after doing this, you will alternate between the frequencies of 65 and 75 MHz and 76 and 108 MHz.

How to Modify Transmit Power

Assume you are attempting to communicate with someone more than 100 miles away. Despite being able to hear each other, the other party claims that your transmission is weak and obscured by background static. By raising your power output in this situation, you can make your broadcast stand out from the background noise and make it easier for your intended audience to hear you clearly.

You can use the UV-5R in both Low-Power and High-Power modes. You must first switch to Channel Mode in order to alternate between the two.

By pressing the orange "VFO/MR" button on the radio's face, you can do this. Hit the button with a hashtag and a key once you are in channel mode. It is located on the radio's face, in the very bottom right corner. You will alternate between Low and High Power by doing this.

It only has an impact on transmissions. That has no impact on getting messages. In other words, going to High Power might help you send a message farther, but it won't help you hear a message coming from a distance.

Raise Or Lower The Squelch Level.

Your UV-5R's squelch level can be adjusted from 0 to 9. The standard setting is set to 3. You must do the following to fine-tune the squelch setting on your UV-5R:

- Press the "MENU" button.
- From here, utilize the up and down arrows to get to "0 SQL". This is where you adjust the squelch.
- Press "MENU" to select such.
- Use the up and down arrows to set the squelch where you desire it to be.
- Press the "MENU" button to confirm your decision.
- Press "EXIT" to exit the menu.

How to Secure a Keypad

You might need to put your UV-5R in your pocket or be in another position where pressing the radio's buttons by accident could mess up your current settings. The keypad can be locked in this situation. By doing this, all of your radio's keys—aside from the three on the side—will be locked out (where the push-to-talk button is). Press and hold the button in the bottom right corner of the radio's face to lock the keypad.

To lock everything, press and hold that button for two seconds. Press and hold the same button once again for two seconds to unlock the keys.

How to Check Frequency

It can be useful at times to simply scan over frequencies to see if you can get in touch with anyone. This can assist you spread your information as rapidly as possible in a catastrophic situation in a foreign setting. When in Channel Mode, FM Broadcast Mode, or Frequency Mode, you can scan.

Simply hold down the "*/SCAN" button for two seconds to scan these frequencies. The radio will scan for a signal once you do this. The scanning procedure will then completely halt until you reengage it. You must first press the "*/SCAN" button once and keep it down for two seconds twice before you can restart the scanning procedure. The "*/SCAN" button will allow you to scan through your saved channels when in Channel Mode.

How to Modify Scan Preferences

The UV-5R has three different scanning modes at your disposal. It can be set to:

- Search up until a signal is found, then stop scanning for a period of time when nothing happens on that frequency (Time Operation);
- It can either scan until it detects a signal, at which point it fully stops scanning until you instruct it to again.
- Scan until it detects a signal, at which point it resumes scanning as soon as that signal quits (Carrier Operation) (Search Operation).

Hit the "MENU" button first to switch to any of these scanning choices. Next, press the "1" and "8" keys simultaneously. Once more, press the

"MENU" key. Then, to cycle to the desired scanning choice, use the up and down arrows. Once you've located the one you want, press "MENU" to confirm and save your selection. Then press "EXIT" to leave this menu.

How To Simultaneously Monitor Two Frequencies

It's possible that your Baofeng UV-5R instruction manual does not mention this, but the radio can simultaneously monitor two frequencies. This could be useful when trying to get as much information from the field as possible or when you have two "rally frequencies" and are unsure which one the opposing party will use (e.g. a disaster operation). Dual watch functionality describes this capacity to simultaneously monitor two frequencies. The Baofeng UV-5Rs feature a dual watch feature.

You need to press the "MENU" button first

before you can enable or disable Dual Watch Mode. Next, press the "7" key. The "MENU" button should be pressed to select Dual Watch Mode. Then, to enable or disable Dual Watch Mode, use the up and down arrows. Once you've made your decision, click "MENU" to confirm. After that, press "EXIT" to leave the menu.

On the other hand, your UV-5R will automatically set itself to transmit on that channel anytime one of your chosen frequencies for Dual Watch Mode becomes active. If you are listening to a frequency that you are not allowed to transmit from, you should be careful about this (e.g. police frequencies).

How to Alter the Color of the Backlight

Maybe you don't like the UV-5R radio's display screen's default backlight color. You can alter it to your preferred hue. To begin, press the "MENU" key. When you are in Standby Mode, receiving a transmission, or broadcasting, you can alter the color of the backlight. Then, after pressing the "MENU" key, you must do the following:

- To change Standby Mode color, hit the "2" key followed by the "9" key.
- To change receive color, hit the "3" key followed by the "0" key.
- To change transmit color, hit the "3" key followed by the "1" key.

Once you've decided which area you want to modify the color for, click "MENU" to choose. Next select the color you want by pressing the up or down arrow. Once you've finished, click "MENU" to confirm and preserve your selection. To leave the menu, press the "EXIT" button.

How to Increase the Memory of the Radio's Frequencies

You can store a variety of frequencies, power output, group signaling information, bandwidth, and other details for numerous separate "channels" on the Baofeng UV-5R. It is only possible to set the ANI and S-Code IDs of a certain frequency using appropriate computer software. You won't be able to manually enter that data. Only when operating in Frequency Mode with the upper frequency (the "A" frequency) set are channels able to be saved.

By pressing the "VFO/MR" button on your radio's face, make sure you are in Frequency Mode before starting to establish a new stored channel. Then, choose the frequency you want by either manually entering the frequency on the keyboard or manually scrolling using the arrows in that direction.

If the frequency you want to save is on a simplex channel, take the following actions:
- Press the "MENU" key.
- Press the "2" key followed by the "7" key. You'll see the display read MEM-CH.
- Press "MENU" to select this option.

- Use the up and down arrows to then select the appropriate channel that you would like to store the frequency as.
- Press the "MENU" key to confirm your decision.
- Then press the "EXIT" button to exit the menu.

A duplex repeater is used by a duplex channel. A repeater essentially functions as a tower that receives your transmission and then launches it further away. Your broadcasts can now go considerably farther thanks to this. With a duplex repeater, signals are simultaneously transmitted and received.

You must configure your radio such that it can both transmit and receive on various frequencies while operating on the same memory channel if you wish to utilize a duplex repeater. In other words, if you've configured Channel 7 as a duplex channel, you must be able to use it for both transmitting and receiving simultaneously.

How to Get Rid of Saved Channels

Do you wish to remove a frequency that you previously added? To get rid of them, follow to following steps:

- Press "HOLD' button
- Enter the channel number you want to delete
- Press "Pgm/E"
- Scroll down to "Delete Channel"
- Press "Pgm/E"
- Select 'Confirm" and hit "Pgm/E"

How to Transmit a 1750 Hz Burst

Prior to connecting to many repeaters available, you'll frequently need to perform this. The repeater becomes accessible to incoming traffic during this exact burst, enabling you to spread your message farther. You must simultaneously hit the "BAND" key and hold down the radio's push-to-talk button in order to deliver a 1750Hz burst.

Enabling Hands-Free Use

You can operate your UV-5R hands-free. The name for this is "VOX." For hunting expeditions, paintball matches, and other activities, this can be beneficial when connected to a headset. It enables you to simply speak while having the radio broadcast your message. You never even had to hit the push-to-talk button for any of it to happen. It is entirely hand-free. Your UV-5R is set to have the VOX turned off by default.

Follow these steps to activate VOX:

- Press the "MENU" button.
- Utilize the up and down arrows to get to option "4 VOX."
- Use the up and down arrows to both select the sensitivity of VOX and to turn it on or off.
- Once you have made your decision, hit the

"MENU" button to confirm.

- Then hit "EXIT" to exit the menu.

Troubleshooting BaofengbUV-5r Common Problems

The radio won't turn on

Causes.

- It has a low battery. Incorrect installation of the battery.

Solution.

- Recharge or replace the battery. Reinstall the battery after removing it.

The battery runs out rapidly.

Causes.

- The battery has expired. The battery isn't fully charged

Solution.

- Purchase a new battery. Power up the battery

The speaker is mute, but the LED indicates reception.

Causes.

- The volume is too low. any DCS or CTCSS enabled

Solution.

- Increase the volume. To communicate effectively, adjust your CTCSS or DCS to theirs. or deactivate CTCSS or DCS.

My transmission is not audible to others.

Causes.

- They don't have your CTCSS or DCS settings. You two are too far apart.

Solution.

- To match your peers, adjust your CTCSS

or DCS settings. Move closer.

Without touching the PTT, the radio transmits.

Causes.

- The VOX is turned on. The VOX sensitivity is excessive.

Solution.

- Turn off VOX. Reduce the VOX sensitivity.

Important Baofeng Radio Accessories

The UV-5R and BF-F8HP are two of the most well-known amateur radios produced by BaoFeng. They can be purchased for as little as $25, and occasionally they are even less expensive in volume. These are standard items in bug out bags and on plate carriers all around the world due to their affordability and features. Despite the fact that ham amateurs frequently mock them, they are nevertheless widely used and inexpensive due of their shortcomings.

Alden Summers Jones recently experienced a diabetic seizure while hiking on a mountain outside of cellular coverage, demonstrating the value of BaoFeng radios. When he came to, he used his BaoFeng handi-talkie to call a nearby repeater for assistance and was eventually rescued.

The BaoFeng radios come virtually fully equipped out of the box, including a battery, antenna, belt clip, wrist strap, earpiece, and charger. Nevertheless, there are a few essential extras that can increase the utility of your BaoFeng handi-talkie in the field.

Below are a selection of cool accessories and devices that go well with Baofeng radios may be found in the rows below.

1. BaoFeng tactical antennas

Although the UV-5R's antenna isn't outstanding, it works for these applications (the one included with the BF-F8 is much better). The fact that it is short enough to avoid poking me in the face or obstructing my path is also important.

For your tactical requirements, you might want to have a look at some additional antennas. A stubby antenna like the Diamond SRH805S is one choice. But, they get out of the way, and if you're in a real-world tactical situation, you might want to keep your signal as local as possible to prevent interception. Stubby antennas are bad for range.

You might think about using a longer antenna on the other end of that, like the Nagoya NA-771, which is a lot longer than the antenna that comes in the box. The benchmark for BaoFeng antennas is the NA-771. The Signal Stick is another fantastic choice. It has the advantage of being flexible enough to knot into a loop, making it easier to fit in a backpack or on a plate carrier.

2. External audio for BaoFeng radios

You wish to find a hassle-free approach to operate the radio. The push-to-talk earpiece that comes with BaoFeng radios is fairly rudimentary. These are quite flimsy and uncomfortable, but they do the job. You might as well rip off the padding over the ear insert to spare yourself some frustration because it comes off so easy. Because they are portable, might be useful.

You probably want something a little more durable for a tactical loadout. This acoustic earpiece, in my opinion, is an inexpensive yet worthwhile improvement from the one that comes with it. The PTT button is larger and more durable, the soft earpiece is considerably more comfortable, and you may attach the mic and PTT button to your clothing. That specific earpiece has the advantage of being soft enough to fit comfortably beneath ear protection earmuffs.

It performs the job. Once you put on the plate carrier, you have a communications setup that is ready to go thanks to the tactical BaoFeng staying in a pocket on the carrier and the speaker mic staying fastened to the strap. The speaker might reveal my location or allow someone to overhear my conversations, which is a drawback. But let's face it, that entire scenario is quite rare. If we get to the stage when those concerns are valid, I'll just switch out the shoulder mic for the headset.

3. Accessories for go-bags

Your thoughts change a little bit when you carry a BaoFeng in your go-bag. Although tactical communications may need the use of a radio, your overall communication goals differ.

- You need a longer antenna since you might need to dial a far-off station for assistance.
- You want a device with a longer battery life because you don't know how long you'll be on the go.
- Also, you need to be able to continuously charge the battery.

Although you may have a Nelson Antenna roll-up slim jim, there are some wonderful options to extend your range if you decide to maintain an antenna like the Nagoya NA-771 on your radio. Moreover, N9TAX manufactures a reputable roll-up antenna.

These antennas fold up into a compact loop and are lightweight, making them ideal for your go-bag. To use them, you'll need a slingshot or roll of twine, a nut, and some cordage, as well as a technique to launch a line into a tree. As soon as you've secured your line to the antenna's end loop, you may lift the antenna as high up the tree as you can without it touching anything else, and then you can attach it to your radio.

These antennas have the drawback of not being very mobile. They work well when you've made a camp, but you can't use them when you're running.

4. A neat BaoFeng pouch

There are several radio pouches available, but our own Tom Rader recommended the ITS Tactical 10-4 Radio Pouch, of which he is a great admirer. Be aware that it is made to fit a

BaoFeng with an installed extended battery.

It can mount on almost anything, including a belt, a piece of PALS/MOLLE webbing, or even a shoulder strap, which is something to be appreciated about it. Also, it folds open so that you have complete access to the radio's controls. To utilize the radio, you can just as quickly pull it out. In order to prevent loss, the ITS 10-4 Radio Pouch can even be fitted with an optional lanyard and retraction mechanism.

5. BaoFeng in your vehicle

You can still use your BaoFeng while driving, but a dedicated mobile radio will operate much better in your car. The primary additional item you require is an external antenna. Most radio transmissions are blocked by the Faraday cage-like effect of a car's interior. In your truck, you could use a Nagoya UT-72 antenna, which is one of the best-performing antennas. It uses a magnet to securely fasten to the roof.

A little interior wire management may be necessary to prevent getting tangled in the built -in coaxial cable, although it may be easily routed through your door. The antenna has a SMA-F pigtail adaptor but uses a PL-259 connector. I find it difficult to screw in the SMA connector, so I may eventually purchase one of the aforementioned BNC adapters so I can quickly switch antennas.

A radio mount for the automobile is an additional accessory you might think about. Although there is no specific suggestions, the majority of phone mounts ought to be functional. If you choose to go that route, you might also think about using the speaker mic suggested before to make it simpler to communicate while driving.

While driving, you can use the battery to power your radio, but if you have a BaoFeng battery eliminator, you can spare your battery from deterioration. It has a fake battery that you can plug into your radio to provide it power from the cigarette lighter socket in your car. It only makes sense for lengthy travels because the only drawback is needing to swap the battery for the eliminator when you get in the car.

Kingdom Johnson is a User Guide Research Writer. He writes for Beginners and Seniors who usually need a guide to operate their devices

NOTES

NOTES

NOTES

www.ingramcontent.com/pod-product-compliance
Lightning Source LLC
LaVergne TN
LVHW051606050326
832903LV00033B/4390